CAREER AS AN
ADVERTISING COPYWRITER

IF YOU ARE NEVER AT A LOSS FOR words, consider a career as an advertising copywriter. Advertising copywriting involves all the elements of good writing, including clarity, flow, purpose, and direction. Great copywriters relentlessly go after their audience, tugging at their emotions, pulling at their purse strings.

Advertising copywriters are telling a story. It has to be interesting, informative, draw the audience in, and lead to a satisfying conclusion. As the story is being told, copywriters play to their audience. Factors like age, gender, marital status, lifestyle, family life, profession, income, likes, dislikes, hopes, dreams, problems, and concerns, are all taken into consideration when targeting an audience and crafting copy.

As the copywriter, you establish the mood, set the tone and create the atmosphere. Where do you want to take the audience? What do you want them to feel? Ad writers can make their copy funny, uplifting, inspirational, thought-provoking, poignant, urgent, chilling, shocking, heart-wrenching, informative, or use any of the other myriad appeals that will resonate with an audience.

An advertising copywriter is limited by space and time constraints, so words have to be chosen precisely, to fit perfectly into a thirty- or sixty-second commercial, a few column inches in a print newspaper or magazine advertisement, or part of a computer screen in a web ad. Nothing can be left out, yet there is only room to include a little. It takes a true word magician to get so much into such a tight and unwavering format. Each word has to convey an array of ideas. The copy has to be pithy and to the point. You have just a few seconds to convince your audience to read on or listen further. It all has to be accomplished in a flash, before a person turns a magazine page, switches a television channel, or clicks the mouse to close the ad.

The ad has to be hard-hitting right from the start and carry through to the end. There may be tantalizing artwork and dramatic pictures, but it is all about the words, the clever catchphrase – that's what makes an ad memorable.

You write, rewrite, and start over. Adding words, cutting words, substituting words and rearranging words. Your mission is to write copy that convinces people that they need, want, have to have, and cannot live without whatever it is you are selling.

While an advertising copywriter's work may be seen and heard by millions, the trick is to have the words in an ad connect with each person individually. That is what gets a person to buy what you are selling.

HISTORY OF THE CAREER

IN THE EARLIEST TIMES, THERE WAS word-of-mouth advertising – one person telling another about a vendor or service provider who offered a great deal or did good work. Then, merchants wanted to be able to spread the word about their offerings faster and farther. That was made easier when the printing press was invented in Germany in the 1440s. Handbills could be printed and posted in public places to alert people about something for sale. One of the earliest known handbills appeared in 1472 on the door of a church in London, advertising the sale of prayer books.

About two hundred years later, *The Kingdomes Weekly Intelligencer* in London ran an advertisement offering a reward for the recovery of 12 stolen horses. It was one of the first newspaper ads ever printed, and its success led to other ads for lost animals. Before long ads for products and services started appearing in newspapers throughout Europe.

In 1704, the British colonies in America took a cue from the motherland and ads started appearing in the *Boston Newsletter*. Other newspapers in America quickly followed suit. Initially, ads were just a block of type and could hardly be distinguished from the stories in the newspaper.

Benjamin Franklin, one of the nation's founding fathers and a printer by trade, was an innovator when it came to advertisements. He owned the *Philadelphia Gazette,* and in the 1730s he started writing headlines for the ads that appeared in his newspaper. He set the headlines in bold type and added illustrations and graphics so the ads grabbed the attention of readers. To make them stand out even more, Franklin used more white space in the ads.

When the Industrial Revolution started sweeping through Great Britain in the mid-1700s, and in the United States in the early 1800s, mass production of goods meant advertising was needed to promote mass consumption of those items.

Most early advertising was handled by the individual business placing ads in newspapers. It was not until 1869 that the first independent advertising agency opened its doors. N.W. Ayer & Sons, started in Philadelphia by Francis Ayer, found the right place to advertise a client's product or service. The company even did market research to back up its advertising recommendations.

By 1890, Ayer was operating his business much as ad agencies are run today, developing complete advertising campaigns, from planning to implementation. Ayer did most of the work himself, but in 1892 he created a copy department and hired his first full-time copywriter.

Though advertising was limited to the print media at that time, local newspapers were not the only option for Ayer's clients. National magazines offered advertisers a much bigger audience, and direct mail was also a very popular way to promote sales at the time.

At the beginning of the 20th century, manufacturers went from putting out just one product, to making a line of products, and branding began. Copywriters now had the responsibility of coming up with clever ideas to get customers to remember brand names. One way was to coin a memorable catchphrase.

The catchphrase became even more important with the advent of radio broadcasts in the 1920s. Advertisers could pick up a national following over the radio with a catchphrase that people simply could not get out of their heads.

Television raised the stakes even higher in the 1950s. Now a product could be demonstrated to a wide range of viewers, but it was the slogan connected with the product that customers would repeat in their heads when they went into the store. That slogan, jingle, catchphrase, or motto was the work of an inspired copywriter, finding a clever way to get a product name recognition. Copywriters came up with catchphrases for companies like these famous examples:

Avis "We try harder"

Volkswagen "Think Small"

Burger King "Have it Your Way"

Timex "It takes a licking and keeps on ticking"

Nike "Just Do It"

Wheaties "The Breakfast of Champions

The 1970s, '80s, and '90s put great demands on copywriters, not only to create unforgettable catchphrases, but also to coin phrases that conveyed the personality of the products and the people who used them.

Today, technology has created new methods and media for advertising, and the words written by copywriters have an impact on a global Internet audience. As more print publications transform to websites, advertising in the digital medium will continue to challenge the ingenuity and creativity of advertising copywriters.

WHERE YOU WILL WORK

AD AGENCIES OFFER THE MOST employment options for writers with a knack for putting persuasive words together. There is a wide range of ad agencies, from small ones that just handle local clients, to giant firms with international accounts.

Very large, well-established advertising agencies often have offices in more than one location so they can be close to their biggest clients and to major media markets. This also allows them to attract a broad spectrum of clients. The larger the agency, the more well known its clients and the media outlets used.

The range of an agency's clients may depend on the focus of the firm. Some agencies have a very general client roster that runs the gamut from authors to department stores. Other agencies specialize – their client list concentrates on a particular industry or sector, like food, arts and entertainment, automobiles, or communications. There are also agencies that have established themselves in niche markets, like computer games or travel and leisure.

Public relations firms and marketing agencies also employ advertising copywriters. These companies offer public relations expertise, and create an advertising campaign to coincide with and complement the total marketing program. They are a one-stop shop for clients who are looking for a variety of promotional services.

Newspapers, magazines, cable-television networks, radio and TV stations, and websites usually have advertising departments with copywriters who can turn a prospective advertiser's ideas for an ad into catchy words that will attract customers.

Major corporations often maintain an in-house advertising department, usually located in their corporate headquarters. Because these companies manufacture a number of products, they want people who work directly for the company to write and design their ads. An in-house staff knows the company, its customers, and how to appeal to the core audience. It also allows the corporation to coordinate its advertising campaign with related work being done in its public relations and marketing departments.

Big box stores, and restaurant and hotel chains, also tend to have copywriters on staff in their main offices, helping to create ads and the coupons and special event announcements that go along with the advertisements.

Large nonprofits, from charities to nongovernmental organizations, looking for just the right words to attract donors and supporters, use the services of copywriters as well.

An increasing number of advertising copywriters are in business for themselves. These freelancers work in their own offices and provide a less expensive alternative to hiring a full-service ad agency. They give clients a go-to person when they need copy written by a professional. Some advertising agencies hire freelance copywriters occasionally, to help handle overflow work during peak seasons.

THE WORK YOU WILL DO

EVERYONE HAS BEEN INFLUENCED by the words of an advertising copywriter at one time or another. Without even realizing it, when shoppers go to the store looking for an item – detergent or toothpaste, for instance – and don't know which brand to buy, the words they remember from an advertisement can lead them to choose one brand over another as they scan the shelves stacked with products. It is the job of an advertising copywriter to put the words together for an ad that will rattle around inside consumers' heads for years to come. The goal is to convince shoppers to at least try the product.

Right now words are being written for an advertising campaign about a product you have never heard of. If the campaign goes well, the product will become a household name. If there is a slogan you will remember, a catchphrase you will say, a copywriter has left an indelible mark on you.

Advertising copywriters are given the responsibility of making the public aware of a product, and getting them to trust it as well. Good copy accomplishes that and much more. Copy makes the sale, and sales drive the marketplace.

Inspired copy is the result of a great deal of hard work. The process starts with research. Copywriters have to be thoroughly knowledgeable about the subject they are writing about. Learning everything about the product, service, or company that is the focus of the ad is a must before the copywriting phase begins.

Part of what a copywriter needs to know can be gleaned directly from the client. Interviewing the client and finding out how and why a product was developed, how the need for a service was discovered, or why a company was started, all provide vital pieces to the puzzle that will eventually come together to form the copy for the ad.

Insights are also gained by delving into the client's own market research. Other data is gathered through independent sources and studying the client's competition. The research may also involve drawing on your own life experiences. You are a consumer. So how does the product, service, or company you are writing about influence your own life?

Only after you have collected all that information can you begin sorting through the findings and organizing them. You can absorb and ponder what you have learned and begin to formulate what you want to include in the copy. There are many considerations. For starters, copywriters decide what the basic appeal of the ad is going to be. That could include prestige, power, comfort, convenience, pleasure, health, security, and a whole host of other persuasive themes that are on the minds of consumers.

Most advertisements have more than one basic appeal. For instance, say you are writing copy for a battery advertisement. Through your research you find that the batteries to be promoted in this ad have a longer life than any other battery on the market, and that makes them not only reliable, but cost-effective as well. In addition, they are environmentally friendly. There are several appeals here and they can all be included in the copy, according to what your research revealed is most important to a consumer who is looking to buy batteries.

Another vital point of any ad is highlighting what makes the product or service distinctive. From your research you know what the competition has to offer, and your job is to tell shoppers what sets your product apart, what makes it better. Why should a customer who is using another brand switch to the one in the ad you are writing? Is the product you represent safer, stronger, and more powerful than anything on the market now?

In the case of the batteries, for example, the strong selling point might be that your batteries can be stored in an unopened package for seven years and still remain fresh, ready to use any time the need arises – they will not let you down in an emergency. You are not selling batteries – you are selling security and peace of mind. There is an old adage in advertising, "Sell the sizzle, not the steak," meaning concentrate on the benefits of the product, not its features.

Are you writing copy for a product or service that solves a problem? Suppose your client manufactures a lubricant that loosens wheel lugs, making changing flat tires on cars easy. No more struggling with a tire iron, trying to turn wheel lugs that just will not budge. In the ad, the copywriter identifies the need and how it is met. This ad is selling a solution.

Every ad has a central theme, a major selling point. Sometimes it is obvious, but many times a copywriter's research will reveal another idea, something a client may have overlooked or may not have realized is even more enticing to consumers. This may change the entire focus of the ad, and it may be the single fact that makes this a winning advertising campaign. Say a drugstore chain wants to advertise that its stores are open with a pharmacist on duty 24 hours a day, seven days a week, including holidays – a good selling point. In your fact-finding, you discover that, as a matter of company policy, the pharmacists on duty at this drugstore chain always check to see if a new prescription interacts badly with any other medication a customer is already taking. You suggest featuring this point in the ad because it shows a high level of caring and concern not found at other drugstore chains (some of which are also open 24 hours).

Copywriters also have to determine who the consumer is – the target audience. That often helps determine the ultimate direction the ad will go in, the points that will be highlighted, the wording that will be used. An ad aimed at a younger audience may be trendy, using slang and contemporary jargon. One for an older audience may take a calmer, more reassuring factual track.

Once you have all your facts together, meetings with the entire creative team are held to exchange ideas and develop an advertising strategy and campaign for the client. These meetings eventually result in a central theme or idea that will be used for the ad campaign. The team decides whether a slogan or catchphrase will be used. Not all campaigns go this route, but if yours does, you are the one who thinks of it – several, in fact, in case the client does not like your original idea. All your research and fact-finding will be distilled into that one slogan or catchphrase, in which you will try to convey everything you want the consumer to know about the product or service.

The ad campaign may have a long-range theme that you help craft. This is an idea that will be used now and carried through over a number of years. The strategy here is to develop a concept that will spark consumers to recall the product or service just by mentioning something having to do with it. MasterCard's "Priceless" campaign, which began in 1997, is an excellent example of a long-range theme campaign. Here is how the original ad went: "Two tickets: $28. Two hot dogs, two popcorns, two sodas: $18. One autographed baseball: $45. Real conversation with 11-year old son: Priceless." After the ad started running for a while, just the mention of the word "priceless" brought MasterCard to mind. Copywriters working on this campaign have come up with many additional versions over the years.

The creative team debates the overall approach to the ad. Should it be lighthearted, whimsical, warm, emotional, straightforward, or extremely serious? The copywriter writes the ads based on the approach the team decides on.

What psychological triggers to use are also up for discussion. A copywriter might end up writing copy for a variety of approaches to show the client how each one would play out. Copywriters go through umpteen drafts until the final phrasing is decided upon. Visuals will dictate some of the words as well. The creative team has to mesh the words with the visuals.

Throughout the process, copywriters can never lose sight of the story they are telling. Everything that is done has to work well with that story. If you tell a good story, the reader or viewer will get absorbed in it.

Once everyone on the creative team is happy with the ad, it is taken to the client. At this stage the copywriter might have to make additional revisions if the client wants to tweak the ad. There could even be some major changes and rewrites made at this point. It is the job of the copywriter to keep working with the wording until everyone signs off on it to the final form. Completion of the ad could come down to finding just one more word or phrase to wrap the whole project up, and the copywriter has to get that done. This might require going back over all your research to locate the missing link – sometimes a painstaking process, but very exhilarating once everything finally falls into place.

While copywriters work on large campaigns with ads that appear in a variety of media, they also work on single ads for an individual medium. They may work on advertisements that are only going to appear in print, be heard on the radio, shown on television, or seen online. Each of these requires different wording that will attract the reader, listener, or viewer.

Experienced advertising copywriters are often asked to work on branding projects. Perhaps the fewest words a copywriter ever writes for a project, branding is one of the toughest assignments. It involves coming up with a name or a trademark for a product or service. Like ad copywriting, branding is about thinking of the right word or few words to convey to the consumer through a product's name what the item is. Brand names – like Jell-O, Kleenex, Xerox, and Scotch Tape – have to be original, memorable, easy to pronounce and something that sticks in the public's mind, conveying a specific image. Some, like those mentioned, are so successful that over time they become synonymous with the type of product. This can actually be a problem for the company, which must be vigilant to distinguish its product from competitors.

Writing packaging copy is also a job for an advertising copywriter. You are trying to get a great amount of information in a small space. When consumers pick up a product they have never purchased before, the words on the package will most likely get them to buy the product. This is another one of those projects where words are written and rewritten in an attempt to get just the right message across to shoppers. Package copy may contain nutrition facts, ingredients, and directions for use, as well as product claims, such as that it cleans as it waxes.

Other types of pieces that advertising copywriters work on include flyers, posters, billboards, and direct mailers. Even in this electronic age, direct mail is still a very popular way of making a sale. Many advertising experts feel that is because getting something in the mail seems to help establish that personal relationship between the seller and the buyer that has always been at the core of advertising. Direct mail projects give copywriters the chance to write something directly to the consumer. Instead of writing "Drive a Chevrolet today," as you might in a general ad, direct mail copy might read something like, "Mr. Jones, you can drive a Chevrolet today. Your car is waiting for you at your local Chevy dealer, located at 123 Main Street. Call Bob to make an appointment."

STORIES OF ADVERTISING COPYWRITERS

I Am a Copywriter in a Corporate Advertising Department

"Though many corporations use an outside advertising agency, the company I work for has always had an in-house advertising department. The company finds that it has more control over the advertising campaign this way. With an outside agency, the company never knows who is going to be assigned as the account executive, the copywriter, the art director. Are they going to be as familiar with the products and the company as someone here in the corporate headquarters? Are they going to care as much? Many of the people who work on advertising in house have been with the company a long time. When new people come in, we really take the time to mentor them because we know they will be stepping into our jobs one day, and we want them to know the inner workings of the company and the advertising campaigns. I know the company, the products, and how the products are made. I actually use many of the products myself. This is my one and only client, and I am totally committed to the company.

It is easy to write about these products and tell people what you want them to know. The company makes beauty and health aids. We make products people always need to buy repeatedly. We take a rather conservative approach to advertising. By that, I mean we do not do a hard sell. We simply emphasize all the pluses of our products and what they can do. The goal is for you to know our products are out there and to think about them when you need a beauty or health aid.

We know are products are good and will do what we claim in our advertisements. We have good shelf placement in the stores. So the objective of our advertising campaigns is for a customer to remember what the product does so it stands out as the eye glances over the array of products stacked on store shelves. 'Oh, yeah. This is the one I heard about,' is what we want customers to say to themselves.

We accomplish that with consistency. We are always out there advertising. We have a very steady ad program. It maintains our customer base and grows it incrementally. The great thing about having a complete product line is that we constantly have the company name out there, front and center, for people to see and remember.

Sometimes we like to say people will eventually grow into our products. Our products are for everyone, but a younger crowd – college students, for instance – will usually just grab the cheapest product of its kind off the shelf, or the one with the hippest looking packaging. There will come a day when those same people, a bit older now, are looking for quality, something that works really well, even though it costs a bit more. They will turn to the old standard they have heard about for years, a trusted name, and we will be there for them.

You tend to keep those customers for the rest of their lives. When it comes to the way we advertise, an axiom that springs to mind is patience. It pays off."

I Am a Freelance Advertising Copywriter

"After working 19 years as a copywriter at an advertising agency, I decided to become a freelance copywriter. It was a tough decision to make because when you work for an advertising agency you earn a steady income. That is not always the case as a freelancer, but I saw a niche market out there that I wanted to try to tap into.

Advertising agencies do not take every client that comes along. They usually look for clients that have a sizable advertising budget, like $500,000, a million dollars, or more. Advertising budgets depend on how much money the client is going to spend on ad placements. The reason is the agency makes commissions on how much the client spends on advertising, so it's not worth it if there are not going to be big media buys. There may be additional fees for the copywriter, art director, and the rest of those working on the ad campaign, but the big budget item is the cost of media. That makes it hard for small businesses that do not have the money to buy many ads to get the services of an ad agency.

That is where I come in as a freelancer. I write the ad copy for these small businesses. Their actual ad budget really does not concern me. I don't place the ads. I just do the copywriting. The clients I work with can buy as many or as few ads as they want. I charge a fee for my work and my job is done.

Mine is a volume business. You do a lot of writing for a variety of clients at one time so you can maintain a steady flow of income. That is a bit different than a large ad agency where the creative team may work on one client's ad campaign for months, or even longer. As a freelancer, you are looking for a quick turnover.

Naturally, there is much more freedom as a freelancer. As a copywriter employed by an agency, you have no say over what clients are brought in. As a freelancer, you have complete control over the clients you take. Of course, you have to go out and find those clients, which is something you do not have to worry about at an agency.

I have more face-to-face contact with the client as a freelancer. When you work directly with a small business, you usually deal with the owner. When you write copy for an ad agency for a large corporate client, you are going through layers of management until you actually get to the person who is going to say yes or no to the copy you wrote. Everyone along the way may love what you wrote, but that one person can turn it down and you have to start over. It can be frustrating not having that instant one-on-one give-and-take with the person who is going to make the final decision about your work.

I like doing smaller jobs and moving on. I like the variety of clients I have and being able to write about a wide range of products, services, and events."

I Am an Advertising Copywriter for an Ad Agency

"I know people who are very sensitive and protective about everything they write. If you are, this job is not for you. You have to be able to take rejection. It's nothing personal. Some days they love everything you write and every idea you have. Other days, well, not so much.

I keep a book with all my ideas. If one client does not like something I wrote, I'll rework it and another client might love it. I look at it like clothes on a rack. Somebody comes in and sees a blouse on the rack and hates it; another person comes in and loves it. You come up with many ideas for each client. Even if the client loves all of them, you are only going to use one or two, and you store the others away – maybe use them on another campaign. Eventually, someone is going to love that idea you had about the singing cow.

You have to realize that not every campaign will be a winner. Some ads never catch on and you do not really know why. It could be that the ad didn't resonate with people or the product didn't. Maybe the product was too expensive or the timing of its release was off. Nobody really knows why one ad strikes a chord with the public and why another one doesn't.

Some of our most successful campaigns were not what we considered our best or even our most creative work. It does not matter. The client liked it and the product sold. It's great when you have a success. It is really awful when you have a failure. It casts a pall over the entire office. If that does not make you want to have a winner every time out, nothing will. You cannot let either your past success or failure control your next project. We worked just as hard on our successes as we did on the campaigns that didn't go so well.

Our clients have a great deal at stake and we do too. In this business, the competition knows our agency is handling a particular ad campaign and we do not want to fall on our face. We put everything we've got into every ad campaign and we are all very committed. When we succeed, and I stress we, it is a shared success throughout the entire agency. If an ad campaign does not go well, we all dropped the ball. No individual credit here, or blame, either. We are all in it together and you have to be comfortable with sharing the accolades and the criticism."

PERSONAL QUALIFICATIONS

MASTERING THE WRITTEN WORD IS essential for copywriters, but it is not the only skill you need to compete in this world of snappy catchphrases and persuasive selling.

Copywriters must be able to draw on an endless supply of ideas. Today's idea is old tomorrow in the fast-paced advertising industry. You have to keep coming up with something new and fresh. There is little time to go through dry spells. By cultivating your ability to think on your feet, quickly developing a novel approach, or by instantly creating an enterprising new strategy, you become extremely valuable in a business always on the lookout for the next big thing.

A vibrant imagination allows you to envision your ideas in action, vividly explain them to others, and champion your cutting-edge concepts. Your advertising campaigns must be innovative, daring, and bold. They push the envelope but are not over the top – you know how to strike that delicate balance.

Copywriters have to understand people. Knowing who you are writing to and being aware of what motivates people to buy something, are valuable assets. You are practicing the art of persuasion.

As part of a creative team, copywriters are usually partnered with other writers, graphic designers, account executives, and art directors. In this field, you need to have a constructive exchange of ideas and work well in a team atmosphere.

Good communications skills are essential. Copywriters have to be able to communicate their thoughts to their coworkers, clients, and the public. They also have to be good listeners, especially when they are talking to clients. The information you elicit from clients helps you write the copy for their advertisements.

As a copywriter, part of your job is to interview clients to learn as much as you can about their company, products, services, competition, and the customer base they want to reach and attract. Knowing the right questions to ask makes your job easier. That requires doing some research. Copywriters need to have a thorough knowledge of the products, services, and industries they are writing about.

All the information copywriters gather needs to be organized. When you are writing, it saves time to have all the data you need at your fingertips. Organizational abilities will serve any copywriter well and will help other members of the creative team do their jobs better.

A copywriter must be an astute consumer with a finger on the pulse of the marketplace. You are familiar with the latest buzzwords and how to plug them in. What gets shoppers hearts racing and blood flowing never escapes you. What consumers want to know about a product comes through in your copy – whether it is all natural, energy-efficient, made in America, nonfat, low-maintenance, economical, just released, or guaranteed to make wrinkles disappear.

ATTRACTIVE FEATURES

MANY PEOPLE WONDER IF THE WORK they are doing really matters. As an advertising copywriter, you know you are having an impact. You are selling something. If people are buying it, you are driving the market.

Copywriters are an essential force in the promotional world. They develop the trends. This is a job that is always relevant. Through their persuasive words, copywriters convince people what sneakers they should wear, what soap they should use, and what car they should drive. Your words are on people's minds when they are making decisions in their lives, and that makes what you write timely and important.

Advertising copywriters work in a creative atmosphere every day. They get a chance to exchange imaginative ideas with coworkers. As a copywriter, you can follow an idea from its inception until it is successfully implemented.

Working behind the scenes, you see how a raw concept is refined, developed, and tweaked on its way to a public debut. You can measure the public's reaction to your work, so you get feedback about what you are doing, even without people knowing it.

In what other field can you walk down the street and watch someone react to the copy you wrote on a billboard, or catch someone out of the corner of your eye pointing to a poster in a train station with a catchphrase you thought of, or glance over at a passenger on a bus reading an ad you authored that is appearing in a popular magazine, and see the expression on her face?

Advertising copywriters are image makers and, therefore, play a meaningful role in the marketplace. You have input on how products are going to be marketed and who is going to be targeted as buyers.

Like all writers, advertising copywriters are storytellers, and there is an audience out there waiting for their next story. Each story is different, with its own twists and turns, and the topics vary. Copywriters develop plots, characters, and settings, and can have their work played out before large numbers of people.

In copywriting, every word you write matters. Each word has a purpose. Nothing you have written that ultimately makes it into an ad is wasted – space is too precious. There is no other writing job that is like that (except maybe poetry). That is why, when you have put together exactly the right words in a piece of copy, you get such a feeling of accomplishment and fulfillment. It is a word game, a puzzle that only those with this unique talent for brevity with the written word can solve.

This is challenging work, not the kind of job that ever gets boring. Copywriters usually have to come up with several ideas for each ad, approaching the subject from various angles and giving the client different options for how the advertisement might read. Each client tests your creativity. You always feel as though you are using all your skills on every assignment because the competition is so keen. Copywriters learn something from every client and every campaign, and that helps them write even better copy in the future.

UNATTRACTIVE FEATURES

UNLIKE SCREENWRITERS FOR TOP-grossing movies, award-winning playwrights, and best-selling authors, advertising copywriters who pen those ingenious ads you see everywhere get very little recognition for their work. There are no credits or bylines on advertisements, so even the most successful copywriters work in anonymity, with no public acknowledgment for their memorable slogans, unforgettable jingles, and treasured characters.

Advertising copywriters have to be satisfied with knowing that it is their work everybody is talking about. There are no autograph signings or crowds of adoring fans for advertising copywriters. These writers pretty much stay in the background, except when those within the advertising industry acknowledge their work.

As an advertising copywriter, you have very little control over the fate of your creations. There are many levels of people who have to approve your work, and copy may be tweaked, changed, and reworked many times, often by people who will readily admit they are not writers themselves. There can be no pride of authorship in advertising copywriting. You have to have a thick skin and realize that criticism of your work is not a personal attack on you.

Ideas are shot down all the time in brainstorming meetings. That does not mean the ideas are not good, just that they are not right for a particular client or campaign. It is part of the business, and something copywriters have to get used to and be able to move on from quickly. The likes and dislikes of clients are often based on their personal tastes. The goal of everybody at an advertising agency is to please the client, even if there is not complete agreement on the final choices the client makes.

The deadlines copywriters face may be extremely tight. This can put them under intense pressure. You have to be able to think of ideas and write under stress. While some campaigns can have long lead times, others can have very fast turnarounds. Even ads that are worked on for months may undergo major revisions at the last minute.

As an ad campaign nears the final deadline, copywriters are often asked to put in long hours to complete the project, which means night and weekend work. At busy ad agencies, this may happen on a regular basis, and it may have an adverse impact on your personal life.

At times, copywriters are asked to write about products they do not particularly like or approve of. This must not show in your work, and most of the time, copywriters are not in the position to turn the job down. Copywriters must be able to put their own feelings aside and write the best copy they can, regardless of how they personally feel.

Like most writers, those who come up with the words for advertisements go through unproductive periods. With deadlines looming, professional copywriters have to push through these tough times and produce top-notch copy despite dealing with writer's block.

EDUCATION AND TRAINING

THOSE HIRING ADVERTISING COPYWRITERS want someone with a college degree, but there is not only one type of degree all copywriters must have to break into the field. You have plenty of options when it comes to what you could major in. There is only one mandatory requirement – the ability to write. With that in mind, many prospective advertising copywriters get a bachelor's degree with a major in English. Attending a college with an excellent writing program, like Emory University in Atlanta, Johns Hopkins University in Baltimore, or Washington University in St Louis, is a big plus.

A bachelor's degree in creative writing is another possibility. The University of California-Riverside and Belhaven University in Jackson, Mississippi, are two of the many colleges with these programs.

Some students pursue a degree in journalism or some other type of media or communications major. Many of the colleges known for their journalism or communications programs also offer courses in advertising. For instance, the University of Georgia's Grady College of Journalism and Mass Communication in Athens, which is known for its variety of degrees in journalism and other communications disciplines, also has courses in advertising and awards a bachelor's degree in the subject.

Northwestern University in Evanston, Illinois, long known for its journalism program, offers a post-baccalaureate certificate in advertising. The certificate is designed for students who want to become advertising copywriters, as well as account executives and art directors. The courses stress the creative aspects of the advertising world, and applicants must have some background in writing and research before being accepted.

The University of Missouri School of Journalism in Columbia, awards a bachelor's degree in strategic communications with an emphasis on copywriting.

At Purdue University in West Lafayette, Indiana, students can earn a bachelor's degree in communications with a concentration in advertising. The advertising concentration explores the planning and creation of advertisements, with courses on focus-group research and advertising theory.

Kansas State University in Manhattan has a journalism program with a sequence just on advertising for students who want to specialize in that field.

Boston University's College of Communication offers a Bachelor of Science in Communication degree with a concentration in advertising. The school also features an AdLab, where students work with advertising veterans and actual clients, learning the business firsthand. Clients pay a nominal fee for AdLab students to develop advertising campaigns. As an added bonus, the clients use those ads to promote their products and businesses. AdLab is the largest student-run, full-service advertising agency in the world. Students can get a Master of Science in advertising from Boston University as well.

Michigan State University in East Lansing has bachelor's, master's, and PhD degrees in advertising. This extensive curriculum includes copywriting, along with many other advertising specialties, such as media planning, consumer behavior, and international advertising. The University of Texas at Austin also has a complete array of undergraduate and postgraduate degrees in advertising.

The University of Illinois College of Media awards Bachelor and Master of Science degrees in advertising. At the University of Central Florida in Orlando, students can get a bachelor's degree in advertising by taking courses like advertising theory, ad design, campaign methods, and media management.

Keep in mind that not all advertising degrees stress writing or even the creative side of the business. Many of the courses cover topics like media management, campaign techniques, production methods, and advertising theory. They give good insights into the advertising business, but they do not specifically hone writing skills. If you need to strengthen your writing skills, be sure to take courses that focus on the written word. This would be in addition to the classes needed to get your undergraduate degree in advertising.

The reason some students who want to be copywriters get advertising degrees is so they have a complete understanding of all aspects of the field. It gives them additional options if they want to venture from copywriting into another facet of advertising. Other areas of study that work well for aspiring copywriters are public relations, marketing, broadcasting, business, and psychology.

A two-year associate degree in advertising and marketing communications is available from the Fashion Institute of Technology in New York City, as is a bachelor's degree in the subject. The instruction includes courses in English composition and copywriting.

Some copywriters choose to attend vocational schools, like the Minneapolis School of Advertising, Design & Interactive Studies in Hopkins, Minnesota; the Houston School of Advertising; or the Miami Ad School, with campuses around the world, including New York and San Francisco. These schools specialize in the creative side of advertising and design, and are aimed at prospective copywriters or art directors. Many of these schools have two-year programs and give students a chance to build a portfolio and make contacts in the advertising world, along with the opportunity to learn the business from advertising insiders.

EARNINGS

THE BIGGEST VARIABLES IN THE salaries of copywriters are the size of an advertising agency and the location. Bigger agencies usually have big-spending clients and more of them. Agencies in large cities usually attract clients with sizable ad budgets, and that enables the agency to pay their copywriters more. The same is true when it comes to salaries for advertising copywriters who work for a public relations or marketing firm. The bigger the operation, the higher the salary is likely to be. Even big corporations with internal advertising departments pay better than smaller companies that have copywriters on staff.

Beginning copywriters average about $35,000 a year at smaller agencies, with starting salaries roughly $45,000 at the more prestigious firms. After about five years, a midlevel copywriter may earn a yearly income in the $50,000 range at boutique agencies and $65,000 at larger ones.

At the highest level, experienced copywriters with a solid record of accomplishment command salaries of about $85,000 at a small agency, and over $125,000 at big agencies. The pay scale for copywriters is about the same at corporate in-house advertising departments.

Most freelance copywriters charge an hourly fee, though some do have per-project rates. The per-project rates come down to an estimate of how many hours you think you are going to have to put into a job. Hourly rates range from $50 to $150, with an average of about $85 an hour. Experience usually dictates the rates a freelancer can charge, as well as the market. Hourly fees charged in bigger markets are higher.

HAVE IT YOUR WAY®

OPPORTUNITIES

NEW YORK CITY ADVERTISING EXECUTIVE Bruce Barton (1886 - 1967) who built Batten, Barton, Durstine & Osborn (BBDO) into one of advertising's leading agencies once said, "In good times, people want to advertise; in bad times, they have to." That means advertising is always a necessity, and that is good news for advertising copywriters.

There is a constant demand for good copywriters, especially those with a track record for coming up with unforgettable slogans and memorable advertising campaigns. It is a competitive world, with more companies vying for the consumers' dollars than ever before. The best way to expand a customer base is through effective ads, and advertising copywriters play an important role in that effort.

Technology has created many new ways of getting advertisements to the consumer. The internet requires specially created, or at least modified, ads. This applies to both stand--alone websites, and web versions of print media. That translates into employment opportunities for advertising copywriters, as businesses across the board must maintain their public profile in the new high-tech world.

Experts predict a growth of about 15 percent in the advertising field generally over the next decade, and that includes positions for copywriters. As the client base for advertising agencies expands, that creates jobs for copywriters. Small businesses are expected to grow dramatically over the next 10 years, and those enterprises will rely heavily on advertising to let the public know they are out there. The expanding small business sector presents a whole new crop of clients for advertising agencies, resulting in increased openings for copywriters.

The proliferation of small businesses also makes it possible for copywriters to break out on their own and find plenty of freelance work. Some start-ups will not have the money to hire full-service advertising agencies, yet they will still want to advertise and have ads that are written by professionals. Who can they turn to for help? An enterprising freelance advertising copywriter.

One of the fastest-growing segments of the copywriting field is freelancing. Being a freelancer gives you the chance to specialize in what you do best, which is writing. Freelance copywriters do not have to deal with any other aspects of the advertising process, like ad placement or even ad design, if they decide not to include them in the services they offer. They can stay focused strictly on writing. Besides, clients might want to handle other facets of their advertising program themselves, like buying space and placing ads, to save some money.

Taking only the jobs they want is one of the reasons people decide to become freelance copywriters. That gives them the freedom to work with clients who have smaller budgets, like nonprofits, that big advertising agencies might turn away. Independent copywriters can choose to represent businesses that sell only environmentally friendly products or products the freelancer has a particular interest in writing about. There is also the option of growing your freelance advertising copywriting business and taking on additional writers and clients, or just keeping it small.

The computer age gives copywriters the chance to get work from literally anywhere in the world, as telecommuting has become very popular with people looking to hire freelance copy pros. As a result of telecommuting, independent copywriters can do work on a wide range of projects, building a strong résumé and portfolio, which are extremely helpful in getting new clients.

GETTING STARTED

ANYONE LOOKING FOR A JOB AS AN advertising copywriter, including those trying to break into the field, needs a "book." A book is an advertising industry term for a portfolio of your work. It is a collection of all the ads you have worked on, including those that appeared in print, on radio and television, and online.

Most copywriters also have a "reel," an archaic term for a compilation of the radio, television, and website advertisements they have done, as the work actually sounded or appeared. Of course, today this is presented on disc, or more effectively on the copywriter's own website. Being able to show samples of the work you have done is extremely important during job interviews for a position as a copywriter.

Internships, especially at advertising agencies, are the easiest way to start compiling your book and reel. Do not wait until you get out of school to get an internship. See if you can land one while you are still attending classes. This will give you some real-life insights into the field of advertising copywriting. Copywriters should not just latch onto any type of internship at an advertising agency. Try to get a copywriting internship. That is the only way to learn the art of copywriting and build the portfolio you need to get a job. Even if your ideas are not used, you can include them in your book to highlight the kind of work you can do. In addition, if you get an internship as a copywriter, there are people in the department who can teach you a few things. You might even find a mentor.

At some of these internships, you have to be somewhat aggressive. If you do not get a copywriting assignment, ask the creative director if there is something you can work on, even just on a trial basis. The purpose of the internship is to learn, and that can only be accomplished by getting in the trenches and trying your hand at actual copywriting.

It is good for interns to get to know everyone in the ad agency, from art directors to account executives. The more people who know you are around, the greater the chance that someone might suggest you for an assignment, if a job needs to get done and the rest of the staff is overloaded with work and cannot do it.

Many advertising agencies have weekly status meetings to discuss current projects. If you are an intern, this is a good place to be. You learn about the advertising campaigns being planned and you might pick up some of the overflow work. Remember: your goal is to build a portfolio.

Another way to put together a book is to create some ads on spec, as if you were writing an actual ad. This is a common practice, and it is an accepted way for people seeking to break into copywriting to present their work when they want to be considered for a job. It showcases your creativity, ability to write, ideas, and approach. You can pick any product or service you want to create an ad for on spec. This is basically a platform for your ingenuity, an opportunity to go after a job by advertising your talents.

ASSOCIATIONS

■ **American Association of Advertising Agencies (4A's)**
http://www.aaaa.org/Pages
/default.aspx

■ **American Academy of Advertising (AAA)**
http://aaasite.org

■ **International Advertising Association (IAA)**
http://www.iaaglobal.org

■ **World Federation of Advertisers (WFA)**
http://www.wfanet.org/en

■ **Interactive Advertising Bureau (IAB)**
http://www.iab.net

■ **International Association of Business Communicators (IABC)**
http://www.iabc.com

■ **Professional Writers Association**
http://www.prowriters.org

PUBLICATIONS

■ **Advertising Age**

■ **Adweek**

■ **International Journal of Internet Marketing and Advertising**

■ **International Journal of Advertising**

■ **Journal of Advertising**

■ **Journal of Advertising Research**

■ Journal of Current Issues & Research in Advertising

WEBSITES

■ Ad Council
http://www.adcouncil.org

■ Advertising Research Foundation (ARF)
http://www.thearf.org

■ AdNews
http://www.adnews.com.au

■ Advertising Educational Foundation (AEF)
http://www.aef.com/index.htl

■ The Professional Copywriters Association (PCA)
http://www.the-pca.org

■ Association of National Advertisers (ANA)
http://www.ana.net

www.ingramcontent.com/pod-product-compliance
Lightning Source LLC
Chambersburg PA
CBHW070230210526
45168CB00019B/1596